W9-AJP-864

Wor

World Book's Learning Ladders

Things I Like

PUPPET SHOW

WORLD
BOOK

a Scott Fetzer company
Chicago
www.worldbookonline.com

WORLD BOOK

233 N. Michigan Avenue
Chicago, IL 60601
U.S.A.

For information about other World Book publications, visit our Web site at
http://www.worldbookonline.com or call 1-800-WORLDBK (967-5325).

For information about sales to schools and libraries, call 1-800-975-3250 (United States);
1-800-837-5365 (Canada).

Library of Congress Cataloging-in-Publication Data

Things I like.
      p. cm. -- (World Book's learning ladders)
   Includes index.
   Summary: "Introduction to common hobbies and
character development using simple text, illustrations,
and photos. Features include puzzles and games, fun
facts, a resource list, and an index"--Provided by
publisher.
   ISBN 978-0-7166-7743-7
   1. Hobbies--Juvenile literature. I. World Book, Inc.
GV1201.5.T45 2011
790.13--dc22
                                    2010026717

World Book's Learning Ladders
Set 2 ISBN: 978-0-7166-7746-8

Printed in China by Shenzhen Wing King Tong Paper Products Co., Ltd.
Shenzhen, Guangdong
1st printing December 2010

Editorial
   Editor in Chief: Paul A. Kobasa
   Associate Manager, Supplementary Publications:
      Cassie Mayer
   Editor: Brian Johnson
   Researcher: Cheryl Graham
   Manager, Contracts & Compliance
   (Rights & Permissions): Loranne K. Shields

Graphics and Design
   Manager: Tom Evans
   Coordinator, Design Development and Production:
      Brenda B. Tropinski
   Photographs Editor: Kathy Creech

Pre-Press and Manufacturing
   Director: Carma Fazio
   Manufacturing Manager: Steven Hueppchen
   Production/Technology Manager: Anne Fritzinger

Photographic credits: Cover: © Corbis/SuperStock; WORLD BOOK illustration by Q2A Media;
Shutterstock; p2, p4, p11, p21, p22, p26, p27, p28: Shutterstock; p5, p6, p7, p17, p20: Getty
Images; p9: Landov; p10, p12, p13, p16, p23: Alamy Images; p19: AP Photo

Illustrators: WORLD BOOK illustration by Q2A Media

What's inside?

This book tells you about different activities people like to do. Some activities are performed by groups of people. Others are performed by individuals.

Things I like

People like to do all kinds of things. Some people like to play sports. Others like to paint pictures or listen to music. Some people like to do all of these things! What we like to do makes up part of who we are.

Some people like to do things in groups.

Some people like to play musical instruments. This woman is playing the violin.

Some people like to do things by themselves.

Some people like to
do things outside.

Some people like to play with
their pets.

Some people like to do
things inside.

⚽ Sports

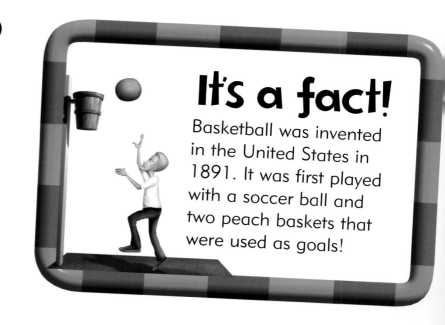

Sports are a great way to have fun and stay healthy. Many sports are played with teams. Sports like golf are played by individuals. The children shown in the big picture are playing basketball.

It's a fact!

Basketball was invented in the United States in 1891. It was first played with a soccer ball and two peach baskets that were used as goals!

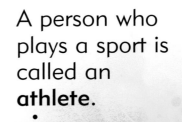

A person who plays a sport is called an **athlete.**

The Olympic Games are some of the most important sports contests in the world. Athletes from around the world compete against one another at the Olympics.

This player has good **coordination**. He can throw the ball into the net while running.

Diving is an exciting water sport. Divers leap into a pool from a bouncy board or from a high platform.

This player is fast. She tries to block the other player from scoring a point.

A **referee** makes sure the players follow the rules.

Basketball players must have good **endurance** to run up and down the court.

Dance

Dance is the movement of the body to music. Some people dance as a profession. Others dance to have fun. The dancers shown in the big picture are practicing ballet.

Dancers must be **strong and flexible**.

Dancers must have good **balance**.

Dancers perform together in a **troupe**.

Many cultures have their own form of dance. Traditional Japanese dancers wear colorful costumes. They use fans as part of their dance.

Dancers often wear **costumes.**

It's a fact!

People aren't the only ones who dance. Many kinds of birds perform dances to attract their mates!

Playing music

People make music to express their feelings and ideas. Some people play music with other people. Others like to play music on their own. People who play musical instruments or sing are called musicians.

A person who writes music is called a composer.

A **musician** must practice to learn how to play a song.

Musicians perform together in a **band.**

A **conductor** teaches musicians how to play a song together.

A **soloist** is a musician who plays part of the music by himself.

Electronic instruments use electric power to make the sounds louder. Many rock bands use electronic instruments.

11

Acting

For actors, the world is a stage! People who act bring characters to life for other people to enjoy. Actors work together. Some actors use the help of a puppet or doll to tell their story.

It's a fact!

In Ancient Greece, actors wore masks. The masks helped the audience understand each actor's part in the play.

A performance takes place on a **stage**. ....

People have used puppets as a form of theater for thousands of years. Puppeteers control the movements of the puppet with their hands or with strings.

Actors tell a story through the speech and actions of their characters.

Puppets can be made of anything—even old socks!

Actors use **props** to help tell the story.

PUPPET SHOW

Many theater actors love the thrill of performing in front of a live audience.

Hobbies at school

We practice many of our hobbies at school. How many different hobbies are shown in this picture?

14

Words you know

Here are some words that you read earlier in this book. Say them out loud, then try to find the things in the picture.

stage   musician   athlete
troupe   costume   band

Drawing and painting

Some people like to make pictures. Pictures may represent their feelings or the world around them. Artists make pictures with lines, color, and shading.

Artists paint on many kinds of **surfaces**. ....

Paintings of natural settings are called **landscapes**. ....

An **artist** may use paints or draw with charcoal, ... crayon, or pencil.

Many artists practice drawing in a **sketchbook**.

Some artists make objects we use every day, such as this teapot.

The way an artist arranges things in a painting or photograph is called **composition**.

Photography is a form of art. Professional photographers may take photographs for magazines and newspapers.

It's a fact!

Thousands of years ago, prehistoric people made paintings on cave walls.

Reading

Reading can take you on many new adventures! People may read to learn how to build or fix things, to enjoy stories, or to learn about other people and places. Reading also helps us develop ideas and beliefs of our own.

Libraries contain many books. They are sorted into sections.

Some books can be read on a **computer**.

Nonfiction books contain information about a certain topic.

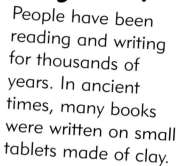

It's a fact!

People have been reading and writing for thousands of years. In ancient times, many books were written on small tablets made of clay.

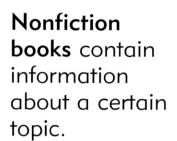

Fiction includes short stories and longer stories, called novels.

Many people like to write. This author is signing copies of her book.

Building forts

In any home, a table and a blanket can become a magical fort! You may use a fort as your own private space or invite others to join in the fun.

People have built forts for thousands of years. Forts served as protection against enemies.

You can **decorate** your fort any way you like.

A fort can be made from old cardboard boxes or other objects around the home.

Working together makes building the fort much easier.

Architects design buildings where people live and work. Buildings shape the landscape of cities and towns.

It's a fact!

Fort is short for *fortified,* which means "made strong."

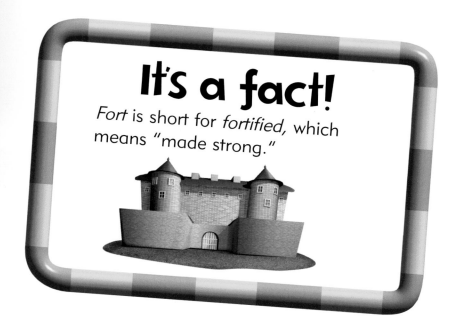

Building a fort is like a puzzle. You have to plan how to fit the pieces together.

Camping

Many people who love the outdoors go camping in the woods. Experienced campers know how to survive in the wilderness for days or weeks at a time. Camping gives you a chance to take in the beauty of the natural world.

Warm clothing is needed for the cool nighttime air.

Many people like to take hiking trips. Hiking is a healthful way to get exercise and have fun, too.

Hiking boots help you walk safely on rocky paths.

Fishing is a popular outdoor activity. Some people like to fish in rivers or streams.

A **tent** offers shelter for sleeping.

Backpacks can be packed with food, water, clothing, and sleeping bags.

23

Hobbies at home

These children are doing their favorite hobbies. What are your favorite hobbies?

24

Words you know

Here are some words that you read earlier in this book. Say them out loud, then try to find the things in the picture.

tent
book

fort
artist

computer
canvas

What is the fort made of?

Did you know?

The author J. K. Rowling began writing stories when she was 6 years old. She later wrote the Harry Potter books.

Soccer is the world's most popular sport. In the United Kingdom and many other countries, soccer is called football or association football. The word *soccer* comes from *assoc.*, an abbreviation for "association."

The music of Africa is based on rhythm and uses drums as the main instrument.

Ballet was invented in Italy during the 1400's.

Sudoku is the name for the popular number puzzles. The word *Sudoku* is Japanese for "the numbers can be used only once."

A person who practices the arts for enjoyment instead of money is called an amateur *(AM uh chur)*.

Puzzles

Close-up!

We've zoomed in on three people doing things they like. Can you figure out what activities they're doing?

1

2

3

Word jumble!

We've taken words from the book and mixed up the letters. Can you unscramble the letters to identify the words?

1. etnt

2. babsektall

3. ralibyr

4. torf

5. tupepp

6. itanp

Answers on page 32.

Match up!

Match each word on the left with its picture on the right.

1. tent

2. athlete

3. sketchbook

4. computer

5. puppet

6. fort

Answers on page 32.

True or false

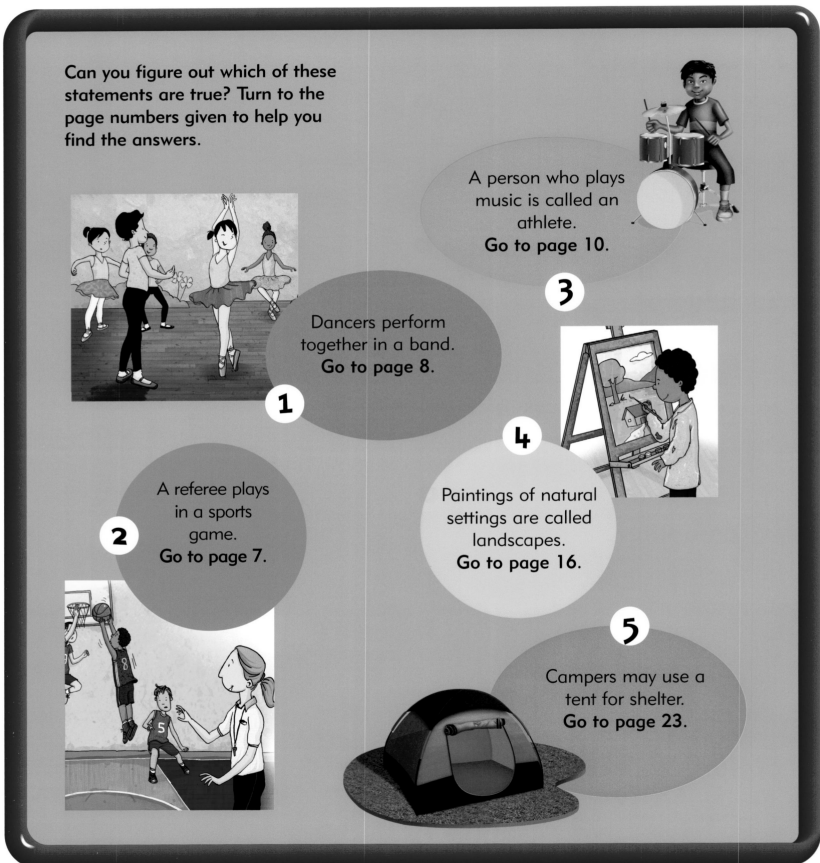

Can you figure out which of these statements are true? Turn to the page numbers given to help you find the answers.

3
A person who plays music is called an athlete.
Go to page 10.

1
Dancers perform together in a band.
Go to page 8.

4
Paintings of natural settings are called landscapes.
Go to page 16.

2
A referee plays in a sports game.
Go to page 7.

5
Campers may use a tent for shelter.
Go to page 23.

Answers on page 32.

Find out more

Books

The Family Book: Amazing Things to Do Together by David Woodroffe (Scholastic, 2007)
This book includes fun activities that family members can do together.

Let's Go Camping by Jan Mader (Pebble Plus Books, 2007)
Learn about the skills, equipment, and safety concerns of camping.

Making Amazing Art: 40 Activities Using the 7 Elements of Art Design by Sandi Henry (Williamson Books, 2007)
Line, shape, form, color, value, texture, and space are the building blocks that all artists use. Learn about these elements through fun activities included in this book.

Sporting Events: From Baseball to Skateboarding by Gabriel Kaufman (Bearport Publishing, 2006)
Discover the origin of our most popular sports.

Web sites

Activities Library
http://www.creativekidsathome.com/activities.shtml
The Creative Kids at Home Web site provides many craft ideas, holiday activities, and science projects that children and adults can enjoy together.

Ducksters
http://www.ducksters.com/
This Web site links you to helpful tips, history, and fun facts grouped by topic into such areas of interest as entertainment, games, hobbies, and sports.

ScienceKids
http://www.sciencekids.co.nz/
Experiments, games, projects, fun facts, and more—all for children who like to explore the world of science.

SI Kids
http://www.sikids.com/
The *Sports Illustrated* online magazine, with articles, videos, and interactive features for young sports fans.

Answers

Puzzles
from pages 28 and 29

Close-up!
1. painting
2. playing music
3. playing sports

Word jumble!
1. tent
2. basketball
3. library
4. fort
5. puppet
6. paint

Match up!
1. b   2. f   3. e
4. c   5. a   6. d

True or false
from page 30

1. false
2. false
3. false
4. true
5. true

Index